Oops & Ohlala
Get Dressed!

Une histoire de Mellow
illustrée par Amélie Graux

Allez !
Je m'habille !

Which socks? The red ones or the yellow ones?

D'abord
je mets
ma culotte.

I'm putting
my jeans on.

Ah ! Le pull,
c'est facile !

But it's inside out!

Can you lace
your shoes?

Tu n'as pas
de scratches?

Je boutonne
mon
manteau.

Zip!
Right up to
my neck!

My hat is too small.

Le mien est trop grand.

Don't forget your gloves!

Ready?

Moi, j'ai des moufles.

On y va !

Oops!

Dans la même collection :

At the Beach!
At the Doctor's
At the Park
At the Supermarket
Bathtime!
Bedtime!
Christmas's Coming!
Dinner's Ready!
Get Dressed!

Happy Birthday!
Happy Easter!
I'm Not Scared!
It's Snowing!
I Love School!
On the Farm
Play With Me!
Tidy Your Room!
Where Is My Cat?

Conception graphique :
Conception couverture : Elsa Le Duff
© Talents Hauts, 2016

ISBN : 978-2-36266-164-8
Loi n°49-956 du 16 juillet 1949 sur les publications destinées à la jeunesse
Dépôt légal : juin 2016
Achevé d'imprimer en Italie par Ercom